my dearworthy darling

This is a work of fiction. Names, characters, places and incidents are either products of the author's imagination or, if real, are used fictitiously.

Cover art: *Whip*, by Zoë Croggon
Copyright © Alison Croggon 2019
Artwork Copyright © Zoë Croggon 2019
Newport Street Books, Melbourne

The moral right of the author has been asserted.

All rights reserved. No part of this books may be reproduced, transmitted or stored in an information retrieval system in any form or by any means, graphic, electronic or mechanical, including photocopying, taping and recording, without prior written permission from the author.

Any performance or public reading of these plays is forbidden unless a licence has been received from the author or the author's agent. The purchase of this book in no way gives the purchaser the right to perform this play in public, whether by means of a staged production or a reading. All applications for performance should be addressed to the author, c/- her agent, Jenny Darling and Associates.

ISBN-13: 978-0-6480676-9-6

First published by Newport Street Books, Melbourne, 2019
newportstreetbooks.com

A catalogue record for this book is available from the National Library of Australia

my dearworthy darling

and other texts for theatre

ALISON CROGGON

Newport Street Books

Alison Croggon is an award-winning novelist, poet, theatre writer and critic. She has had sixteen works for performance produced across Australia, including the operas *The Riders* (score by Iain Grandage, Malthouse Theatre/Victorian Opera 2014), winner of the Vocal/Choral Work of the Year in the 2015 Art Music Awards; *Mayakovsky* (score by Michael Smetanin, Sydney Chamber Opera, 2014), shortlisted for the drama prize in the Victorian Premiers Literary Awards; and *The Burrow* (Perth Festival 1994). Plays include *Rules of Thumb* (Red Shed 1997) and *Lenz* (Melbourne International Arts Festival 1996). She is also a performance critic, and in 2009 was named the Geraldine Pascall Critic of the Year. Her selected critical essays, *Remembered Presences*, was recently published by Currency Press.

Alison has released nine collections of poetry. Her poems are widely published in journals in Australia and internationally, and are included in many major Australian anthologies. Her first poetry collection, *This is the Stone*, won the Anne Elder and Dame Mary Gilmore Prizes. *The Blue Gate* was shortlisted for the Victorian Premier's Poetry Prize. *Attempts at Being* was shortlisted for the NSW Premier's Literary Awards Poetry Prize and was nominated for a Pushcart Prize in the US.

She is the author of the acclaimed fantasy series *The Books of Pellinor*, which to date has sold more than half a million copies worldwide and was shortlisted for three Aurealis Awards. Other novels include *The River and the Book*, winner of the Environmental Writing for Children Award and shortlisted in the WA Premier's Literary Awards, and *Black Spring*, shortlisted for the NSW Premiers Literary Awards. She lives in Melbourne, Australia, with her husband, the playwright Daniel Keene, with whom she is co-writing a science fiction series, *Newport City*. A middle grade novel, *The Threads of Magic*, is due out in the UK, the US and Australia in 2020, as is her creative non-fiction book, *Monsters*.

Contents

My Dearworthy Darling   1

The Famine   39

Blue   59

Yellow   95

My Dearworthy Darling

And what do madwomen find in their delirium? The marriage that eludes them.

Catherine Clément

My Dearworthy Darling was first performed in August, 2019, at the Malthouse Theatre as a co-production with The Rabble Theatre, co-directed by Kate Davis and Emma Valente, with the following cast:

WOMAN 1:	Jennifer Vuletic
WOMAN 2:	Natalie Gamsu
MAN:	Ben Grant
VOICES:	Emma Batty, Caitlin Duff, Simran Giria, Tessa Hulsbosch, Kitty Malam, Emlyn Sugden and Gretel Sharp

Note: This is the version of the text at the beginning of rehearsals. There may be changes to the performed version.

Written in residence at La Chartreuse de Villeneuve-lez-Avignon Centre national des écritures du spectacle (National Centre for Performance Writing).

This project has been assisted by the Australian Government through the Australia Council, its arts funding and advisory body.

Part One: The Carpark

1.

A woman kneeling, alone.

WOMAN   How my desire scorches me a flame forcing open every portal of my body

    Each organ of my body blazes I cannot tell if I am more bliss or anguish

    As a tree shakes with the force of the tempest so do I shake with love

    I yearn for the bliss of your beneficence for your love to fall over me like rain a rain of golden light a mist of sweet aromas for the delight of my five senses

    If I could be luminous and pure as the godhead in the pangs of birth a star in the chaos of becoming and no part of me disgusting to you no part of me beneath your grace

    I am burdened and afraid I want to rise into your love and let down the weight of my body until I am the fullness of beauty unbecoming and undone in the agony of my pleasure

    I am listening for you

    I am waiting

2.

MAN	Where did you put it?
WOMAN	I didn't put it anywhere
MAN	You must have put it somewhere
WOMAN	I didn't touch it why would I?
MAN	You probably picked it up and put it somewhere and forgot like you always do you can't keep your fingers out of anything you're a pain in the arse
WOMAN	Where did you leave it do you remember?
MAN	Just here like I told you it was just here
WOMAN	I'll see if I can find it you probably -
MAN	It's like you do it on purpose you're trying to undermine me this meeting is really important and if I don't / have the
WOMAN	I wouldn't do anything like that you know I wouldn't
MAN	I know I didn't leave it at work it was here like I told you and I didn't touch it
WOMAN	I'd know if I had put it anywhere I'd remember
MAN	Would you really know?
WOMAN	Of course I would
MAN	You wouldn't know you forget everything your memory is shot
WOMAN	No wait you were reading it in bed remember you were reading it in bed last night you must have left it in there
MAN	Yeah but then I got out of bed remember I put it here
WOMAN	Did you try looking in your briefcase?
MAN	Oh yes here it is all good
WOMAN	Great
MAN	Okay where's my keys
WOMAN	See it wasn't me
MAN	Shouldn't be late I'll text if there's problems

WOMAN	It wasn't me
MAN	Okay okay gotta run see you tonight

MAN leaves.

WOMAN	It wasn't me

3.

WOMAN   I read today that the earth is burning up and we are turning into poisonous clouds

I read today that tardigrades are also called moss piglets and water bears

I read today that jackboots are back in fashion

I read today that thirty thousand years ago fish hooks were carved from the shells of sea snails

I wonder what I'll do when I'm old but not old enough to be precious

Beat.

I went to the supermarket but I forgot what I went there for I sat in my car in the carpark and I stared out of the car window and all the blood in my veins went still like it was made of lead I was heavier than a planet but empty

I thought to myself I will never feel anything again

I looked out of the window I couldn't feel anything the tarmac sparkled where a beam of light fell across it and there was a baby sparrow hopping about in the sun

It looked so happy cheeping and hopping and I watched it and the heaviness began to lift I thought this is a gift

And then a car turned into the park and that was the end of the baby sparrow a smudge under a wheel one second it was there and then

And I thought of that phrase, not a sparrow falls

But the sparrow still falls

4.

MAN   Best thing was some guy who totalled his car because he ran into a herd of guineapigs I said excuse me? He said yes guineapigs it's true there was a herd of guineapigs on the road and I swerved to avoid them and came off the road I said come off it mate he said no really they just ran out in front of me the lady down the road said some of hers escaped and they bred into a herd I couldn't stop laughing and he got offended his toe was broken plus he totalled his car I guess you lose your sense of humour a bit in that situation but anyway

I mean feral guineapigs is that even legal

Back when I started it was okay I was twenty seven and earning seventy k I didn't mind the hours so much though it's always full on sometimes you're working on maybe two hundred claims at a time

It's okay if there's an office and a car and a pot plant and staff you've got autonomy see what I mean but now well now it's all automated you sit in a cubicle in a headset and the computer works out the liability and damages and the boss is like about fifteen years old and hasn't got a clue and treats us like garbage and office politics fuck me they are poisonous everyone talks about getting out but with things like they are

Most of the time you're the bad guy you're handing out the bad news to some schmuck who didn't read the fucking policy or doesn't understand the law or he's just a conman and people get upset but you keep your cool because you're a professional but sometimes

These days no one is ever in the wrong you have to tell someone who's one hundred per cent sure that your insured is at fault that in fact it's them who are at fault and you're not paying their damages and they get personally insulting and you want to say why don't you jump in the sea you and your car or your house or your dog or your fucking Rolex that you listed as twenty five thousand dollars although you bought it in China for twenty

You stay polite because you're a professional you hear what I'm saying but sometimes

You can't imagine the people who try it on bent lawyers crooked contractors staged car accidents torched pizza shops fake injuries in the end you realise everyone is on the scam nobody gives a fuck it's an eye opener I can tell you I mean people are fucked they're fucking fucked

5.

WOMAN 2	God you'd think she'd at least text yes sugar please
MAN	Maybe her battery died
WOMAN 2	We're going to miss the beginning at this rate
MAN	If we ever actually get there
WOMAN 2	No milk thanks
	Pause.
MAN	Is she punishing me that's what I keep thinking
WOMAN 2	Nah she's just selfish she doesn't care about other people
MAN	It's just that there's been problems lately
WOMAN 2	Well there's always been problems that's what I'm saying
MAN	Do you think so? I mean it wasn't / always -
WOMAN 2	I mean from when she was a kid she was always a bit that way
MAN	Sure / but
WOMAN 2	Self obsessed I mean she always thought that she was the centre of the universe you hear what I'm saying
MAN	But this is different I think it's a sickness she's sick
WOMAN 2	She was always bit of a bully if she felt threatened she used to bully me I'll never forget it
MAN	Maybe you're right though it's definitely got worse since she first went into hospital

WOMAN 2	That's probably the drugs they gave her but let's face it she was always a bit unstable it's not about being sick
MAN	I sometimes think I should put my foot down
WOMAN 2	That's what I'm saying it's time you asserted a bit of control you should talk to her doctor
MAN	I already tried I made an appointment but he wouldn't tell me anything
WOMAN 2	Why not?
MAN	He said it was professional ethics ethics my arse he just wants control
WOMAN 2	You're family that's outrageous it's not like it doesn't / affect you
MAN	I said I wanted to be informed for her welfare not mine I said I'm her husband and I'm concerned
WOMAN 2	Family counselling like I said / you should -
MAN	A waste of time I reckon I just need to know what I'm dealing with
WOMAN 2	You're right but what can you do?
MAN	He could have just told me privately man to man it's for her benefit not mine that's clear I just want to know how to help that's what I told him
WOMAN 2	That's only fair
MAN	He said not without her permission and / she obviously
WOMAN 2	Some people just don't want to be helped *Pause.* All I'm saying is that it doesn't surprise me
MAN	Well I guess you would know
WOMAN 2	We've been sisters our whole lives of course I'd know

6.

WOMAN   I've lost the words

I don't know whether I ever had the words

Either I had them and they were taken away or they don't exist I don't know which

It's like the world doesn't fit there are too many words and they're all the wrong ones and I try to make them fit the sky is the wrong sky maybe even the sky

Or maybe it's that I open my mouth and the world goes deaf I speak and it's as if I'm not saying anything at all or I say the words but they hear different words from the words I said the words they expected to hear maybe and the words I said just didn't happen

So bright and shining in my head shining

7.

VOICES.

- The world is not gentle she said the road is full of stones that tear my skin but even these are not as cruel as people
- I cannot bear this pain she said it is beyond all bearing it is greater than any silence greater than any word it is birthpangs and deathpangs all together

- Why did you leave me she said why am I alone in this hell why
- She said truly I am a dovecote and the wings flutter inside me and outside me they are the wings of love but ah the wings are breaking
- She said truly I desire no hurt

8.

A child crying alone.

WOMAN 2   They're undermining me all the time stealing my work lying to my face some people are like that they just suck you up and spit you out you give them half a chance they'll do you over because they're weak and dishonest and lazy

And meanwhile this situation it's not helping she just tells me that God loves us we will find our way she says that God takes us to his breast and suckles us I mean it's nuts and I say well ok that's all well and good but that's not going to pay our mortgage is it that's not going to pay the bills that's not any help right now and she says oh you of little faith you deserve what you get

I had that nightmare again you know the one where everything's burning the fire is all around us you can see the flames in the darkness a ring of flames creeping closer and closer

It's been years I used to have it all the time as a kid

It's a nightmare I tell you a nightmare I can't sleep for worrying and the stress is getting on top of me I told them I can't work because of the stress you're causing me I have a condition it's the situation and all this stress with the family

And the fires creeping closer and closer until I feel the heat on my face burning my skin off the radiant heat is what kills you you don't even have to be near the flames and in the middle of the fires there's –

No I can't look I just know that in the middle of the fires there's this thing not a monster it's worse than that it's –

I'm the only one who sees the real situation and I'm the one who's concerned and prepared to deal with it not that anyone thanks you most especially those most nearly concerned they turn around and slap you in the face that's just how it is

Nothing it's just nothing

I'm happy to make the sacrifice for the greater good don't get me wrong but after all these years you'd think I'd have earned some gratitude I guess at the end of the day I just have to learn how to put myself first

Like there's nothing there nothing at all just this howling silence this –

9.

MAN and WOMAN.

MAN	That was better than I expected
WOMAN	I really enjoyed it
MAN	Everyone was saying it was shite but it just goes to show you can't trust critics
WOMAN	Yeah they were all saying -
MAN	All the blokes at work they said it was shite
WOMAN	Too much CGI not enough story
MAN	The CGI was pretty cool though
WOMAN	Especially at the end when the planet blew up
MAN	Took a bit long to get there but yeah it was cool at the end
	Pause.
WOMAN	Maybe it's just because we didn't expect anything
MAN	Low expectations that way you don't get disappointed
WOMAN	True
MAN	Like marriage really
WOMAN	*Laughs.* No with marriage you just make sure that you have no expectations at all
	Pause.
MAN	Are you saying you're disappointed?
WOMAN	Disappointed in what?
MAN	In me are you saying you're disappointed in me?
WOMAN	No I made a joke
MAN	You said that you had no expectations of marriage that way you wouldn't be disappointed
WOMAN	See I was saying I wasn't disappointed

MAN	No you were saying that you are disappointed you're disappointed in me
WOMAN	Don't be stupid I / was just
MAN	Who are you calling stupid?
	Pause.
WOMAN	Don't get like this
MAN	Get like what?
WOMAN	Please we were having a nice time / and I just
MAN	You're disappointed and you think I'm stupid I get it
WOMAN	No that was –
MAN	It was what? What was it?
WOMAN	– just a turn of phrase a joke
MAN	The stuff I have to put up with from you and you have the hide / to say
WOMAN	I didn't / say –
MAN	Like what do you do all day I get home after a shit day and you'd think you'd at least have the courtesy to get dinner after everything I do I mean I'm not an unreasonable man you'd /think that
WOMAN	But you know that / I've been
MAN	You'd think that you'd have the fucking courtesy to at least get me some fucking dinner
WOMAN	I do most days but I thought well we're going out / anyway –
MAN	And then you're too fucking tired or you've got a fucking headache or you're just so sad and I'm exhausted after dealing with shitheads all day and I come home and my wife is just this fucking depressive who can't be fucked even to smile let alone get dinner for her sucker husband who works his arse off every day you'd think you'd at least fucking try

	Pause.
WOMAN	I'm sorry
MAN	What's that?
WOMAN	I'm sorry I can't help things sometimes I'm so sorry I'll try to be better
MAN	Do you think being sorry's enough we're all sorry aren't we and it doesn't make any fucking difference we're all fucking sorry

10.

WOMAN	A moment in a dream.

Something has stopped.

I'm not sure what was in motion, it isn't something I was looking at, but the cessation of movement is perceptible even though I can't trace the source. It's like when a forest goes silent when a predator is present, how suddenly there's this stillness as everyone who might be prey becomes still.

It might be a threat to me too but I don't know. Until I trace what has become still and why it has become still I won't know whether it's a threat to me or not. Maybe there's a raptor hovering high up or a feral cat creeping through the undergrowth. They wouldn't be interested in eating me. Maybe it's a curtain that was lifting in a slight breeze and that now hangs still and heavy under its own weight. Maybe it was a dog barking a long way off that has now stopped.

In my dream I am very still. I don't breathe.

Shift, perhaps a double voicing.

- For evyr the mor slawnder and repref that sche sufferyd, the mor sche incresyd in grace and in devocyon of holy medytacyon of hy contemplacyon and of wonderful spechys and dalyawns whech owr Lord spak and dalyid to hyr sowle, techyng hyr how sche schuld be despysed for hys lofe, how sche schuld han pacyens, settyng all hyr trost, alle hyr lofe, and alle hyr affeccyon in hym only.

WOMAN   He began to write in the Year of Our Lord 1436

A short treatise of a creature set in great pomp and pride of the world which then was drawn to our Lord to great poverty, sickness, shames and great reproofs in many diverse countries and places, of which tribulations some shall have been shown after, not in order as it fell but as the creature could remember when it was written, for it was twenty years or more from the time this creature had forsaken the world
Pause.

WOMAN   Not in order as it fell
Pause.
Shames and many reproofs

A marvellous tree of five fruits of different colours and many kinds of leaves. The tree is full of wings and music. Text may be spoken or projected.

- And often tymes, when sche was kept wyth swech holy spechys and dalyawns, sche schuld so wepyn and sobbyn that many men wer gretly awondyr, for thei wysten ful lytyl how homly ower Lord was in hyr sowle. Ne hyrself cowd nevyr telle the grace that sche felt, it was so hevenly, so hy aboven hyr reson and hyr bodyly wyttys, and hyr body so febyl in tym of the presens of grace that sche myth nevyr expressyn it wyth her word lych as sche felt it in hyr sowle.

Part 2: Visions

I.

Scenes from the Black Death.

WOMAN	It must have seemed like the end of the world
WOMAN 2	For a lot of people it was
WOMAN	I sometimes try to imagine what it was like but how can you imagine that a third of the population died whole towns just wiped off the map bodies piling up everywhere
WOMAN 2	But here we are sometimes history is very consoling
WOMAN	You only hear from the people who survived the people who didn't survive don't get to write history do they it makes us unreasonably optimistic I reckon
WOMAN 2	True

Phone rings. WOMAN 2 looks at the number, and silences it.

WOMAN	Nobody ever thinks it will be them who'll end up in the limepit
WOMAN 2	They reckon history is coming back
WOMAN	How can it come back that doesn't make sense
WOMAN 2	I mean that it stopped for a while and now it's started again
WOMAN	But it doesn't work like that the past doesn't stop happening just because someone says so
WOMAN 2	That's what history is it's what people say
WOMAN	No it isn't there's bones
WOMAN 2	And anyway whoever writes the history what do they

know they only know what they know they don't know everything

Phone rings again.

WOMAN	But what if everything is always still happening like with light
WOMAN 2	(*Silencing call.*) What?
WOMAN	The further away you travel the more you can see if you went far enough away you could watch the beginning of the universe they're already doing that with telescopes
WOMAN 2	But it's still over it's in the past that's only traces *Pause.*
WOMAN	I get these moments maybe sitting on a bench in the park when the sun is shining just so when it comes out from behind a cloud all silver maybe or maybe I'm just in the kitchen and I'm baking a cake and I hear a bird only it's just like music playing in my head or maybe just before I drop off to sleep and for an instant just for the tiniest flash of time everything is clear you know those moments when you understand that everything is always still occurring nothing ever stops every moment of the present contains all of the past and it's all still happening
WOMAN 2	That doesn't make any sense
WOMAN	You should listen or you'll never understand anything you have to listen or you'll never see it *Pause.* I can't say it properly I don't have the words but it's like what eternity is *Pause.*
WOMAN 2	Have you told your counsellor?
WOMAN	No why should I?

WOMAN 2	You should tell your counsellor that sounds like religious delusion
WOMAN	It's nothing to do with him it's private
WOMAN 2	I was just saying maybe you should tell him if you don't tell him maybe I should this kind of thing is why you've got problems
WOMAN	But why it's just thoughts it's just things I think
WOMAN 2	It's not normal that's what I'm saying you're not normal

2.

Children cowering under bombs. Refugees fleeing burning cities.

-     I don't know when I am she said
-     And God said there is no when there is only now
-     And she said how can I bear all this now all these eternities so many tears so much suffering now becoming now becoming now
-     I can't bear it she said I could never bear it

3.

Lakes of sulphur and copper blue.

WOMAN 2	Vicious
MAN	Underhand and cunning, that's what it is
WOMAN 2	I don't know how she just doesn't see it
MAN	It's part of the condition I do my best I tell her you don't know what you're doing it's part of the condition

WOMAN 2	But what's the condition?
MAN	The condition she's got
WOMAN 2	Have they put her on medication?
MAN	If they have she's not telling me she's hiding it I had a look but I couldn't find any that's why I went to the doctor but like I said

Phone begins to ring. No one answers.

WOMAN 2	There was that day I'll never forget it she got the pliers out and said put your finger there and so I did and she shut them
MAN	Really?
WOMAN 2	I was five maybe seven anyway it was me got into trouble I'll never forget it it was plain even then the viciousness
MAN	Things like that they reckon they begin early I googled
WOMAN 2	But you never know how it's going to manifest later in life it could be dormant for decades and then suddenly
MAN	There it is whoosh it's in the character
WOMAN 2	Character's what counts in a person in a country we've lost character that's why we're in the state we're in
MAN	You can't argue with facts I mean it's her responsibility at the end of the day but what am I expected to do I go to the office and do my job like everyone else I spend all day dealing with wankers who want something for nothing they didn't read the fine print like sorry you're on a floodplain what do you expect it's inundation you're not insured you should do your due diligence and not be a cheapskate and they're on the phone calling me a cunt like it's my fault not theirs and I come home and I expect at least a bit of respect she has no respect that's what I'm saying
WOMAN 2	You're right it's about respect

4.

Angels weeping in the heavens.

WOMAN   I can look at a baby and see how unhappy it is I can see the bruises inside its eyes I can put my ear to the ground and hear the hollowness that goes all the way down to the centre of the earth I can hear all the gunfire all the bombs all the screams all the people in the world weeping

I sit down at the table and eat my spaghetti with my hands

Everyone pretends not to notice but they do they don't meet my eyes their glances go through me like fishing wire and their silences are as eloquent as if they call me bitch animal barbarian madwoman

Who are you they say with their eyes who are you I can hear them whispering in their minds who are you with bolognaise dripping off your chin and fingers in a perfectly respectable restaurant on a sunny day when people are out with their children having perfectly respectable lunches and not one of the children is screaming I am the only one screaming but the screams are inside my head

Is it contagious they wonder maybe it will spread it's dangerous to children it is certainly a personal threat

It's the fault of her mother it's her fault it's the fault of society it shouldn't be allowed in public in front of people normal people who pay their taxes and have good credit ratings and houses with air conditioning and dishwashers and clean babies why hasn't the government done something

And the waitress comes up and says can I help you and I say I would like some more bread but she doesn't bring me any bread

I can read all those whispers inside their skulls like little scripts of red acid the sharper they become the less I care

Inside me the screams turn into laughter a divine laughter the laughter of angels who are without malice and who see into the hearts of the damned how much they are afraid and have to make themselves safe with their cutlery and laundered table cloths and insurance and chit chat how are you I'm fine how is the baby so big now but all it does is hide the terror how afraid they are of themselves of their sins their indifference and spite

How afraid they are that if they listen to the voices inside them one day if they're not careful they might sit down and eat spaghetti with their hands in a restaurant because they finally understand that cutlery isn't important

It all makes sense at last it all makes sense

5.

The suffering of animals.

- And sometimes if she saw a man had a wound, or a beast, whichever it were, or if a man beat a child before her or hit a horse or other beast with a whip, if she saw or heard it, she thought she saw our Lord being beaten or wounded, just as she saw it in the man or in the beast, either in the fields or in the town, and alone by herself as well as among people

Keening that rises and falls

6.

Wasteland. Armies. Demagogues.

MAN	I told you my address I told you already
VOICE	Calm down sir please tell me the exact situation
MAN	Hurry I don't know what she'll do next
VOICE	Are you in immediate danger
MAN	Not immediate no I have taken steps
VOICE	Do you require treatment
MAN	I am uninjured so far but this may change
VOICE	So please tell me the exact situation
MAN	I'm in fear of my life I am in shock

VOICE	Officers are on the way now sir please be calm are there any injuries
MAN	I don't know whether she's conscious she's not moving
VOICE	Is she injured
MAN	It's hard to say I have taken steps to protect myself she is very aggressive and she seems to have no
VOICE	How has she been aggressive sir
MAN	She has a knife I don't know what she will do next she's on the floor
VOICE	She has a knife on the floor?
MAN	She had a knife before I mean before she was on the floor
VOICE	Was there conflict
MAN	We were discussing the free market I told her it was the only mechanism that ensures freedom and balances the rights of citizens it is a moral force I said and the state must remove its impediments to the free flow of trade and its unwarranted restrictions on the enlightened self interest of the human race under conditions of perfect liberty we would at last attain true equality is what I told her

Knocking.

VOICE	But this doesn't take into account how the free market is totally responsible for the present financial crisis not to mention
MAN	She went off the deep end she went crazy she went for me with a knife I had to defend myself
VOICE	Officers have arrived at your address sir please answer the door

MAN	She never listens she is off in her own little world and now it's
VOICE	*Off* Yes I am in communication with the caller
MAN	I am greatly concerned for her welfare she needs help

7.

Rivers blighted by salt. Chemical mines. Forests burning.

- Sche bot hir owen hand so vyolently
- And also sche roof her skin wyth her nayles spetowsly
- She stood by the side of the road blessing the cars
- She dreamed all day of flames and policemen

Phone starts ringing.

- She crowned herself with flowers with fumitor and furrow weeds with burdock hemlock nettles and cuckoo flowers
- She walked barefoot through the city streets dressed all in white
- She prayed in the department store she shaved her head she wept and the people turned away their eyes they would not look
- She sat down in an office and in front of her sat a row of psychiatrists she lifted her chin
- She said it's not me who's mad it's you

Phone rings out. Silence.

8.

The body carefully opened out and its organs placed on a table.

WOMAN	It's not about fault did I say anything about fault
WOMAN 2	You can't help yourself you just have to be different / like you think
WOMAN	No
WOMAN 2	Like you think that you're better than / everyone else that's what
WOMAN	No I don't mean -
WOMAN 2	Look I'm just trying to be frank I'm trying to be honest
WOMAN	But / I didn't
WOMAN 2	You were in a state I understand that like I said I'm not saying it's your fault
WOMAN	It was just a / misunderstanding he
WOMAN 2	Well you have to take some responsibility
WOMAN	I'm trying to take responsibility I'm trying but I want to be clear about what I'm taking responsibility for I'll take responsibility for what I've done but it has to be something that I've done not something I didn't do how can I take responsibility for that

Phone starts ringing. Nobody answers it.

WOMAN 2	But you said you don't remember what you did
WOMAN	I said that / yes but
WOMAN 2	And what about the knife what were you thinking
WOMAN	What knife there wasn't a knife
WOMAN 2	If you don't remember how do you remember whether there was a knife or not you were in a state

WOMAN	There wasn't a knife
WOMAN 2	I saw the knife it was in your hand
WOMAN	But you weren't there / how could you
WOMAN 2	I saw the knife with these eyes are you saying that I can't see with these eyes I saw it I heard what you said I heard what you were saying
WOMAN	But you were in your house you said that just before he called you and you were in your house folding the washing after dinner
WOMAN 2	He called my mobile I never said I was in my house how do you know where I was you don't remember anything I was there I saw it I don't do laundry on Tuesday anyway
WOMAN	Why / are you
WOMAN 2	Listen I'm trying to be understanding you need help but you've got to stop denying what
WOMAN	I don't need help not that / kind of help
WOMAN 2	You've got to stop denying what's going on I told you I saw the knife you've got to take responsibility for your violent nature
WOMAN	There wasn't any knife / I never
WOMAN 2	You said you didn't remember but I remember what happened I saw that you had pliers in your hand clear as day and you were going to cut his throat you said you were going to cut his throat you were raving
WOMAN	He never said why are / you saying
WOMAN 2	He was in fear of his life for good reason that's what I'm saying you're a danger to yourself and to everyone around you and it's other people get into trouble because of you I've talked to the police that's what they said
WOMAN	They didn't say that to me they gave me a number
WOMAN 2	I mean how did he get cut that's what I'm saying there was blood everywhere

WOMAN	No / that's
WOMAN 2	When you were trying to stab him and he pushed you away and then you / sit there saying
WOMAN	But he wasn't cut
WOMAN 2	Yes he was I saw it how can you / sit there
WOMAN	You weren't even there
WOMAN 2	Don't be ridiculous

9.

The abyss.

MAN	Why won't she speak to me I only want to talk maybe we can work it out if only we could just talk

10.

The scouring of the flesh.

-	The flesh rent open in beast or man the sword piercing the breast the fair skin deeply broken into the tender flesh through the vicious blows delivered all over the lovely body the hot blood running out so plentifully that neither skin nor wounds could be seen but everything seemed to be blood

Part 3: Asylum

WOMAN. VOICES.

- For summe seyd it was a wikkyd spiryt vexid hir
- Sum seyd it was a sekenes
- Sum seyd sche had dronkyn to mech wyn
- Lithicarb 300 mg per day to be adjusted after two weeks
  Active ingredient Lithium carbonate
  Prescription only medicine, or prescription animal remedy
  Side effects: tiredness, loss of appetite, nausea, vomiting, diarrhoea, hands shaking, increased thirst and consequent increased frequency of passing urine, memory problems.
- Sum bannyd hir
- Sodium Valproate 750 mg a day for three weeks
  Active ingredient valproate
  Prescription only medicine, or prescription animal remedy
  Side effects: congenital anomalies, infection, alopecia, thrombocytopenia, nausea, vomiting, abdominal pain, weakness, drowsiness, tremor, flu-like symptoms, dizziness, diarrhoea, and anorexia.
- Sum wisshed sche had ben in the havyn
- Abilify 15 mg once a day
  Active ingredient aripiprazole
  Prescription only medicine, or prescription animal remedy
  Side effects: dizziness, lightheadedness, drowsiness, nausea, vomiting, tiredness, drooling, blurred vision, weight gain, constipation, headache, and trouble sleeping

-	Sum wolde sche had ben in the se in a bottumles boyt
-	And so ich man as hym thowte
-	The cawse of hys malyce was for sche would not obeyn him
-	And sche wist wel it was ageyn the helth of hir sowle for to obeyn hym as he wolde that sche schulde a don

*

WOMAN	Wordlessness is the most beautiful utterance

            The outward part is our deadly flesh-hood which is now in pain and woe

            The inward part looks to its extinguishment in the brilliance of revelation and is not afraid

            The inward part is truth

*

            I call and no one's there where have you gone my love where have you gone

            I thought I was going to die
            I think I will die
            I am dying

            I wasn't afraid at the time I curled up small against the pain as little as I can make myself I don't feel anything at all

	Thus she saw a great brightness so vivid and bright and of such wonderful beauty that it could not be compared to anything the human spirit could imagine
	This brightness was a circular shape and in this brightness there appeared a great red brightness so resplendent and so beautiful that it illuminated with its great beauty all the white brightness
-	And in that white brightness appeared a little child
-	And that child appeared in the midst of all this splendour

*

WOMAN	I'm afraid after only afterwards that's when I realised something was broken
	I thought he's going to kill me if not today then tomorrow or the next day if he sees me he will kill me I couldn't go out into the street because he might see me he might be walking somewhere to the shops or on his way to work
-	On a night as this creature lay in her bed she heard a sound of melody so sweet and delectable that she thought she was in paradise
WOMAN	Panic out of nowhere maybe once a day maybe seven times when I saw a certain yellow that reminds me of

	the colour of the wall or maybe a certain smell a faint smell of gas and desolation or maybe a song I never know when it will happen my heart starts racing I can't breathe I want to run

- This melody was so sweet that it surpassed all the melody that ever might be heard in this world

WOMAN   I ran I thought you would save me where have you gone why have you abandoned me

Phone rings.

- A melody without any comparison, and it caused this creature when she afterwards
- heard any mirth or melody to shed plenteous and abundant tears of high devotion
- with great sobbings and sighings for the bliss of heaven
- not fearing the shames and spite of the wretched world.

Phone stops ringing.

*

WOMAN   Her sadness is the alleviation of all pain
Her adornments are all undressing
Her deepest silence is her sublime song

Silence.

*

Hospital bed. Wings. Birdsong.

WOMAN   I open one eye I open another eye
For the first time I see for the first time
A window floating but there is no wall the window is pregnant and luminous
And outside this window is a new world the sun has never before risen upon this untouched
And holy expanse of cloud and light
A plain of bliss on which my sight may press
Bruiseless and endless

I open one eye I open another eye
My hand clutches a white fabric as chaste as the tongues of angels
My hands are clothed in singing cloud

I touch one hand I touch another hand
I touch every wrinkle every crevice in the skin these hands are a map of banished harm where monsters may walk their heels unbloodied by flint or thorn with no voice rebuking them no scathe of insult no injury no loss

I see a frame of sky I see a vault that encloses me and yet which opens up the most perfect freedoms a wall perhaps that is the parapet of heaven without mark or scar there is a cloud that lifts me and another binds me down there are no sharp edges no edges anywhere

Truly there is no hurt

- Sche nevyr tellyn how swet it wern
- Many white things
- Sweet sounds and melodies
- You will hear things you have never heard
- You will feel
- The fire of love burning
- Voice of a little bird singing
- I am always pleased with thee
- You please me so well
- You may boldly
- In your wedded bed
- Take me as your wedded husband
- As your dearworthy darling and you may boldly
- Kiss my mouth
- My love is ever ready for you
- There is no other comfort but me only
- Which am I
- Your God
- Who am all joy and bliss to thee

8

Naked.

WOMAN I'm here, at last.

The terror of now. The elation of it. It's been a long journey. It's taken my whole life.

Beginnings are brutal.

I don't believe in anything any more. There is nothing else, there is no one else. No one except you.

All of you.

Who are you? Will you betray me?

Will you hold me close beside you, will you let me go, will you never ask me ever to be anything except what I am becoming?

What if you say: no, I will do none of these things?

If you say no I will walk away, down that long white road that is neither remembering nor forgetting, because from now in every moment, no matter how painful that moment is, I will remember joy. Because from now in every moment I will only ever become who I am.

What if you say: yes? What will I do then?

Will I say yes?

Faith, even though I know how easily we are broken. Hope, even though we are mortal, living in the stink of our dying flesh.

Love, which demands nothing and asks for everything.

I will hold out my hand.

Blackout.

Translations of Middle English texts from *The Book of Margery Kempe*

Part 1, Scene 10
For the more slander and reproof that she suffered, the more she increased in grace and devotion in holy meditation of high contemplation and of wonderful speeches and dalliance, when our Lord spoke and dallied to her soul, teaching her how she should be despised for his love, how she should have patience, setting all her trust, all her love and all her affection in him only.

And often when she was kept with such holy speech and dalliance, she wept and sobbed so much that men wondered greatly, for they little knew how homely our Lord was in her soul. Nor could she ever tell the grace that she felt, it was so heavenly, so high above her reason and her bodily wits, and her body so feeble in the times of the presence of grace that she might never express it with her words as she felt it in her soul.

Part 2, Scene 4
She bit her own hand so violently
And she tore her skin grievously with her nails

Part 3, Scene 4
Some said it was a wicked spirit that vexed her
Some said it was a sickness
Some said she had drunk too much wine

Some banned her

Some wished she was in heaven

Some wanted her in the sea in a bottomless boat
And so each man as he thought

Scene 5
The cause of his malice was that she would not obey him

And she knew well that it was bad for the health of her soul if she obeyed him as he wanted her to do

Scene 7
She never told how sweet it was

The Famine

>   ... *the future*
> *you shall know when it has come; before then, forget it.*
> *It is grief too soon given.*
>
> *Agamemnon*, Aeschylus

> *Who are you? Look, I blow out the world,*
> *It will be night, I will no longer see you,*
> *Do you want only light?*
>
> *The Restlessness of the Dream*, Yves Bonnefoy

The action takes place before the doors of a pub.
LIZA is an old woman.

Content warnings:
This text contains racist language and references to Aboriginal massacres.

The Famine was commissioned by the Red Shed Company, Adelaide. It was first performed in July 1997 at the Red Shed Theatre, directed by Tim Maddock, with Annabel Giles as LIZA.

Scene One

Darkness. A loud drumbeat. The lights come up on LIZA.

LIZA   I see him sometimes in dreams. His face pale as whey under the water. His hair waving slow like black weeds.

I can't touch him. That's the worst. He's crying. An old black crow somewhere in my head. He's crying and the wings start. He's crying now. He'll never stop crying.

All that shit I wiped up for nothing. I made things. A little shirt of calico. To keep the sun off. A little blanket. I kept his milk teeth in a bottle. He still had some of them.

All alone in that big dark river.

Pause.

I still got some teeth.

Seven brats and I still got teeth. Dugs? Well. That's asking.

I'm so tired. What I wouldn't give for a place to rest. You got a place? Something to drink? A bed?

I can't remember sleep. Real sleep. Sleep without dreams. I can't shut up. Are you the dead? If it's quiet I start hearing everything. Leave me alone. I can't listen any more it hurts.

There's no time left. It's where we all come at last.

Drumbeat.

I was beautiful. They said. I didn't believe them. Nobody says so any more. I miss it. Those beautiful lies. You get to miss everything in time.

Even him. Bastard that he was.

That poor gin. Remember? Wailing under that tree for hours and hours. Her baby died. He got a cold and died like in a day. A little kid just walking. Her hair all stiff with some kind of fat. It was raining and she was sitting under that tree slashing herself with a rock. Her tits running with blood. And ash in her hair. Everyone left her alone. But she didn't stop. She just went on and on and on and on. And John went out and shot her through the head. Because of the noise.

I was pregnant at the time.

It caused a few problems I remember. But John fixed them up real quick.

When Johnny drowned he said nothing.

I've given up feeling sorry. It never did no good.

Drumbeat.

> My house was cursed
> Every brick every nail
> The crops died in the ground
> Floods rotted the foundations
> Fires choked the cattle
> Old crow famine stalking me
> And all my children sickening

My children.

I was a strong beast. I had them on my own. Some gin come and helped after the first two. The first I was so frightened. It hurt like Christ. John wasn't there. Women's business he said. As if I knew what to do. But I was up the next day. Childbearing hips they said.

Her pulling on my nipples. And the smell of milk and her hand on my tit while she sucked. That cry like a cat. And when her eyes opened up on mine. Nothing ever quite like that.

I didn't mind the shit. I was used to that.

I seen so many dead babies.

Drumbeat.

> Horror piled on horror
> cold hands reaching out
> to cold hands

        eyes dark with blood
        and skulls spilling fear
        over smoking ground

        and all around the silence
        of frightened children
        hiding in the scrub

Drumbeat.

Animals, he said.

I was an animal to him. But I was his animal. I learnt to say nothing.

He'd go and fuck the gins. I knew that's what he did. Some would have been his kids. But they was jacking up. He come in one day in his big boots and slammed the gun down on the table. All the men was outside. We're going hunting he said. For some proper game.

What could I do? I never heard worse but some things as bad some things in the ship maybe some things at the factory but I never heard worse. You think all your wits are dead and then back they come just when you don't want them. What could I do? Some of them was good company. Our kids played together. Not that he knew. He'd have had me if he knew. Animals he said.

He thought he was some kind of king. There wasn't any to tell him different. The king back home? You'd have thought they was milk brothers the way he talked.

His majesty's government never showed me much gratitude. For all I done. Seven years hard labour and transportation. Me and the rats. For soliciting on his majesty's streets. You'd have thought they was the aisle of a chapel the way they talked. Washed out each day with the tears of innocents.

I was going home that night. It was a bad night. A poor night. Sleeting. This man comes up. How much darling he says. Half a crown for the likes of you I says. And they scoop me up like a pile of shit and throw me into limbo.

I was going home.

Drumbeat.

Home.

I'm so tired. Somewhere to lay down. Somewhere to rest. A place where it's all quiet. Mine. You can imagine such a thing. I remember looking through the windows at Christmas out in the snow looking in. Me and the other kids we'd just go and look. There'd be a tree with an angel at the top. An angel like my Mamma. I was just little. I looked and looked and looked.

I had dreams then. I didn't know no better.

Pause.

> love given and love stolen
> love rotting to sorrow
> love wasted and love seeded
> to disastrous flames

Drumbeat.

Mamma?

How'd it get so dark? Mamma? Why is it so dark? Why aren't you talking Mamma? The candle blowed out Mamma I can't see nothing.

What happened what happened

Don't go away. Mamma where you are why aren't you talking Mamma why don't you say something

Mamma

say something

Mamma I'm getting nightmares it's the birds again with their big beaks they're going to peck me all down my back until there's only bone and blood their eyes are big and scary and the hair

o the hair flying around like whips and their eyes burn

Drumbeat.

She bore me. Heavy with me felt me under her heart kicking shuddered under my kicking touched me with her secret smile loved me. And when I cried she held me I remember that.

And then she died. Blood all over the bed and nothing could stop it I tried with my hands and the sheets and the rags and the pillow I tried but nothing could stop it nothing she said Liza she said and then she lay there still and white so white there was no more blood in her

She lay there she said nothing nothing at all

Drumbeat.

It was another baby what killed her. She didn't want another baby. She couldn't hardly feed me. Nine years old I was. Nine years old and all the secrets died and I was afraid I was just afraid all the time.

So much blood.

No blood left in Johnny. Just silence. Blue little boy snagged by the edge of the river with his hair all clotted with mud and lips so blue you'd never think lips would get that blue and a blue face. And his arms and legs white like the belly of a fish. A dead thing.

I picked him up. I carried him home. He was so heavy. Wet and cold and heavy. He smelled of the river. Weeds and mud.

I don't know what the dead dream. All my children. I never knew their dreams. I can't hardly remember them. All gone all my daughters all gone. Rotted away. Mad. I can't stand to remember them except as babies when they was all new and the pox hadn't showed up yet.

They was too good for him. So he give them his blood to murder them with. Like he murdered everything.

Susannah. She was tall like a willow. I thought I never saw such a beautiful young thing out of me I used to wonder. She was so fine too fine for this world. My first. She never learned reading nor writing. But I thought she was like a fall of music music you hear sometimes in your head like angels singing she was like that. The men used to leer at her and me there clutching the frypan I would have killed them and they knew that and they didn't dare. I never knew what she saw. When she was little she'd go climb a tree and you'd call and call and call. I'd beat her I was so beside myself after Johnny. And she'd look at me wide eyed like she didn't understand no fear just this surprise like I'd woken her out of a dream. She never cried. My heart was sore with fear for her I couldn't see how she'd manage not like Vicky or Elaine they was practical girls but Susannah was always somewhere else.

And then the mark and I knew. And I watched her.

She was the first. After each dying the one before seemed merciful. Johnny's was the kindest of all. Dreaming in the river.

I was rough with them I got no choice I was stuck out there in the hut with the trees all around full of the wind sometimes I thought the wind was ghosts in agony ghosts that John murdered come back to tell me and sometimes there was footsteps and no one there and me on my own and all the kids snivelling and the stink of washing and the trees dripping outside dripping blood outside and I couldn't stand it not the trees any more and the wings in the trees and the river calling not any more I couldn't stand it

Drumbeat.

John come home. After Susannah died.

He was never home before.

John come home.

Blackout.

Scene Two

LIZA.

LIZA   Behold thou art fair my love. Behold thou art fair. Thou art all fair my love there is no spot in thee.

                 Let him kiss me with the kisses of his mouth for thy love is better than wine.

Pause.

                 I sleep but my heart waketh.

Pause.

                 my love my love my love

Pause.

                 Customers too much to hope for this end of life. Too old too old. Since time began I've been here. Waiting. And why not? Poxy old whores like me are hard to come by. Mostly they're dead by the time they get as old as me. Too much opium. Too much gin. Old dry bones in the ground. But here I am.

                 Get up you old bitch. I'll call the law. You're driving custom off.

                 Offer me a room I'll get off your doorstep.

                 I ain't got none.

My money's the same as anyone's.

Yeah well show me some.

I ain't got none.

Move on then or I'll break your arse.

You fat old bastard. Time was you would've begged for a sniff of me.

Time was you didn't stink like dogshit.

I ain't got no home.

I seen your humpy down by the river. Down with the blacks.

I ain't got no home.

Who's going to fuck a sad old hag like you?

I ain't that bad.

You get sores looking at you.

They called me the queen of Lambeth Lane. Men turned when I passed. I had a red dress with lace at the bodice and I put a red rose in my bosom. My hair was black as the ace of spades and my eyes was blacker.

Get on home.

Do you remember, Jack? Do you remember when I was beautiful? My skin was smooth as milk. Untouched I was. I walked with my head up high. And the streets. Do you remember the streets, Jack? Lambeth Lane and Huddlestone Street and Scrimshaw Alley and Blackburn Rd and the long drop to Newgate. Streets with doorways so close you could spit. People walking and shouting and the smell of chestnuts roasting in winter and the woman hawking pilchards and the blind old beggar who I give a penny most mornings when I got it. Angie with her bright red hair screaming blue murder down the corridor and the featherbed jig each night. Everywhere the smell of piss. Number eight in that shithole of a room but I bought red curtains red velvet curtains and at night I drew them and felt like a queen.

Get off my doorstep.

I wasn't always of easy virtue. But one thing led to another. Let him without sin like the priest said. Poor old bugger.

It's getting late.

You got a drink Jack?

You've had enough.

Just to see me home. Just to. See me home.

Blackout.

Scene Three

LIZA. *A dog howls in the distance.*

LIZA   Black dog death
                              with his maw hanging open
                              black dog death
                              black dog death
                              come to get his dinner

The dog howls again.

It's cold. It's so cold. How'd it get so cold in the middle of summer? Did you see the fires on the mountains over there? Are they coming this way? The moon like a bowl of blood through the smoke. The whole earth burning. That'd warm me up.

What? John? I can't hear you. What?

Get fucked you fucking whinger.

On and on and on. Like an old woman he is. Liza get this. Liza get that. What's he think I am?

It's so good to sit down. Washing and cleaning and cooking all day. Wiping his arse mostly. Mad as a march hare. All his skin rotting. He stinks. Jesus. It's so cold. Why doesn't someone shut the windows? Is it the fire? Is it blowing this way?

If you don't shut up I'll fucking kill you.

I want to go home.

I'm tired of this shit. Tired do you hear? All my life I've been tired. All my life in chains. I was born that way. And they never come off not ever. Chains all the way to the grave. Some was round my ankles. Some was not.

The stew. It's burning. What a stink.

Let it burn. Who's going to eat it? He just shits everything right out. In out in out it's hardly worth the trouble. I can't hardly eat anything these days it's like I got no space. If I get any thinner I'll fall through the floorboards.

I hate this house. Built out of blood this house is. John built it to die in. It stinks of death. When he wasn't so sick he'd sit on the verandah and take potshots at the crows. I hate crows. Pulling the eyes out of the newborn lambs big fat ugly black bags of doom.

We even got a piano. I dust the fucking thing every day. Lady of the house. I embarrass him. No class. He pulled me out of the shithole and he's stuck with me. I'd run away but there's nowhere to go. Into the bush like those women the silence gets them the fucking silence and one day they just run out in the scrub and never come back. I'm tougher than that. Worse luck.

What's he want of me? I don't think he knows.

Do you love me? I said. Yes he said. I was so lonely. He was gentle. At first he was so gentle. He made me cheap. Because I believed him. I was young and stupid then. Now I'm old and stupid.

He knows I never loved him. He's got enough already to make me feel small. Some things are mine. Not many. Some.

When I look at Susannah I almost remember. A long time ago.

Where'd she go? Susannah? My Susannah. My first. Up that tree again talking to the angels. Can you hear them singing to her? Their robes smell like fire. They burn in the sky. You daren't look into their eyes it'd be like swords going through you.

I'll kill him. I'll kill him one day.

Susannah?

He only come home to die. When I don't need him no more. He never give a shit for me or no one else. And now he's scared. All those times I was afraid. Of him mainly. The blacks is kind to me. I don't have to say nothing. They have this way of disappearing. They know when he's coming before I even hear the gate they just melt away and then I know. Otherwise there's trouble. Or was that before? There's no blacks now. I used to hear them singing sometimes at night not any more.

Nothing any more.

The dog howls.

Kill me, he says. For godsake woman. Put me out of my misery. I can't stand it any more he says. The pain and the stink and the shame. I never saw him beg before. I'm sorry about Johnny he said. And he starts bawling. His nose come off he's got no nose left just a big weeping sore and his ears he sticks to the sheets and the tears dripping off him. And all the men out with the fires I can't move him.

I swear to god I can't stand no more of it. You hate a man all those years and then there's just this big empty howling inside of you like a wind over the desert. It's so easy to be sorry.

If only he'd shut up. Each time I sit down he starts again. Babbling and drooling. Shitting the bed. Out of his mind.

Susannah? Where is that girl? I can't do it on my own. I always did I'm old now I can't lift him I ain't got no strength. I'll leave him there maybe it's for the best.

The fire's coming it won't be long now.

It's so cold.

I'll get a shawl there's a nice one in the wardrobe a red wool shawl makes me feel like lady. I'll make a cup of tea with sugar. Then I'll be all right. It won't be long now.

I'll sit and wait.

Pause.

> Black dog death
> come for his dinner.

Blackout.

Blue

*As soon as one begins to divide things up
there are names;
Once there are names,
one should also know when to stop.*

Tao Te Ching

JED	A man, about 40
RITA	A woman, about 40
RUTH	A woman, about 40
FLOG	A man, about 50
BERN	A young woman
BERENICE	A young woman
WAITER	A young man
OLD WOMAN	

The action is set in a country town.

Note: **RITA** and **RUTH** must be played by the same actor. The **WAITER** and the **OLD WOMAN** should also be a doubled role.

Blue was first performed at La Mama Theatre, Melbourne, in May 2001. It was directed by David Branson, designed by Peter Mumford with sound by Nick Craft, and was performed by David Branson, Louise Morris, Virginia Cusworth, Anna Voronoff and Phil Roberts.

Scene 1

RITA and JED

RITA	It's winter.
JED	I know.
RITA	The sparrows fall frozen and starving on the ground. The sky is the colour of granite.
JED	I know.
RITA	Sometimes the sky is clear. It's a blue of immeasurable distances. I would like to go there, wherever that blue is, but I understand it is only an illusion, that it is no place, only a depth of time travelled by broken light. Light itself has no colour.
JED	I know.
RITA	Blue is the saddest colour. It symbolises how estranged one is from one's own being. If one simply was, one wouldn't have to think. One could be at home in the world. An animal can be at home in the world because it has no consciousness of its mortality. When I was a small child, I thought I would live forever. I thought the sky was a blue bowl God put over the top of the world. I don't think those things any more.
JED	I know.
RITA	You don't know the same way I do.
JED	I'm waiting for you to tell me something I don't know.
RITA	I'm telling you now.
JED	You talk and talk and talk and you never tell me anything.
RITA	I'm telling you something now. I'm telling you something. If you want to be told something, you have to listen. If you know everything in advance, you can't be told anything new.
JED	I wish you could surprise me.

RITA	If you could see me.
JED	I'm looking now.
RITA	If you could see me, perhaps things might be different.

JED looks.

JED	I'm looking at you now.
RITA	You're looking, but you don't see me.

RITA turns away. JED comes up behind her, as if to embrace her, and she leans back into him. He strangles her. Her body falls to the ground.

JED	Now I can see you.

Scene 2

JED on a bus. He is next to an OLD WOMAN. A long silence.

JED	Anything is possible. That's the truth. But none of us want to believe that. I could be anyone. I could be your long lost son whom you've forgotten, whom you bore in shame and disgrace and agony and gave away, long ago when you were a young woman. I could be the shape of a desire you have forgotten, the temperature of the sun on the back of your hand in a moment in a summer when you were a child and you sat on a bench, waiting for your parents, and the sunlight fell on your hand and you waited for your hand to crisp and curl away in smoke and leave a little pile of ashes there on the bench, where you were sitting. I could be the smell of a dream you had last night. Of course, you can't remember your dreams. *Pause.*

Really, I'm nobody.

Pause.

You must have lived a long time. How did you survive it? Now you're invisible. Nobody looks at old women. They inhabit the streets with their shopping trolleys and every now and then an old woman falls over and then people notice, because an old woman fallen over can be the expression of their concern. But in the butcher or in the supermarket, where the old woman counts out her coins for her frozen vegetables, nobody notices her. She doesn't even have a sex. It is just a pair of eyes, looking out on the world, and no one looks at it. I'd like to be invisible. It would reinforce my desired inconsequence.

Pause.

I killed my wife yesterday. I don't remember why. Now I'm going somewhere. I don't remember where.

Pause.

If you could hear me, a lot of things would be different.

Silence.

WOMAN   I can't hear you.

Scene 3

RUTH at a bus stop.

RUTH   I was a bird and then I was invisible.

A long long long time ago. I'll tell you a story. Do you like stories? Good. This is a story.

I was a bird and I made the sky with my wings. Before I flew there was nothing. Not even God. I flew as high as I could because I wanted the sky to be very big.

And it was very big.

Back then I was invisible. Did I say that? I was as invisible as your most secret dream, the dream you have forgotten in your most secret night, where you keep hidden all your most precious things.

And this is the story. Because the angels got jealous. They didn't want anyone to know that I was there before God. And they tricked me with a promise. They locked me in a white van and clipped my wings and put me in a cage where all day long all I could hear was the screams of the damned. And the devils pricked me with needles and made me fat oh so fat as fat as I am now so I wasn't invisible any more and I wasn't beautiful any more. I used to be so beautiful my breasts were as beautiful as Dolly Parton's I had a face like Marilyn Monroe and my wings were made of the most exquisite silk and swansdown but they injected me with fat so I wasn't beautiful any more I looked just like this. I cried and cried o how I cried and they told me to be quiet. So then I was very quiet because I thought that maybe then they'd let me go.

And then did they let me out of the cage and said fly away little birdie. And I tried to fly away I tried and tried but I was too fat. And then they laughed and laughed. I can't stop hearing them laughing. They laughed and laughed and laughed.

It's a true story. The true stories are always the saddest.

Scene 4

A fairground JED and a fairgound attendant, FLOG.

FLOG	Every now and then you have to wipe up the vomit out of the cars. That's the worst job. Some kid full of doughnuts and coke rattling himself to bits. Makes no sense to me. Life would have to be dull to do that for excitement.
JED	I guess so.
FLOG	It's enough to make you wonder. Computers. Nintendo. There was none of that around when we were kids. Bad for the fairgrounds. Kids just stay home these days staring at a screen. What are they learning? How to manipulate their thumbs with accuracy. How to shoot down an alien spacecraft. What good is that? How's that going to get them a job?
JED	Maybe they could be fighter pilots.
FLOG	Not that there's many jobs around anyway.
JED	Or computer programmers.
FLOG	That's not a real job.
JED	It pays real money.
FLOG	Staring at the screen again. Nobody talks to anybody these days, that's the problem. Human relationships. That's the secret. People have to get out and talk to each other.
JED	Are we talking?
FLOG	If we're not talking, what are we doing?
JED	I don't know.
FLOG	They need to get out in the real world. Get themselves dirty. Kids these days have no idea.
JED	Is this the real world?
FLOG	It's real enough.
	Pause.

JED	I need a job.
FLOG	There's no jobs here.
JED	I can clean up vomit.
FLOG	What are your qualifications?
JED	Do I need a bachelor of sanitation?
FLOG	No, what have you done?
JED	Lots of things. Nothing.
FLOG	Can you count?
JED	Usually.
FLOG	My kiddie train supervisor ran away last week to join an accountancy firm. So I'm a hand short.
JED	I can supervise a kiddie train.
FLOG	Safety is an issue. You have to strap the little bastards in before you start the train. You have to keep watching in case little Johnny falls off. We don't look for lawsuits here. It's a duty of care.
JED	I need a job.
FLOG	You look a bit skint.
JED	I slept under a bridge last night so I'm not at my best. Normally I'd put on a tie.
FLOG	There's a spare berth in the caravan. Since Loopy took off.
JED	Loopy?
FLOG	The kiddie train man. One of my best. But he had ambition.
JED	Why was he called Loopy?
FLOG	Figure it out.
JED	Maybe he didn't like his name.
FLOG	He didn't like anything much.
JED	I don't either.
	Pause.
FLOG	We'll do a trial today. You pass, you get the job.
	Pause.

	You need a wash, there's a shower block over there.
	Pause.
	What's your name?
	Pause.
JED	I can't remember.
FLOG	Like that, is it? I have to call you something. You can call me Flog.
JED	Call me nobody.
FLOG	I can't call you nobody. Snoopy, I'll call you Snoopy.
JED	I don't like it.
FLOG	It'll do. For now.

Scene 5

BERN and BERENICE, watching television.

BERN	Anyway, he comes up and says, he says
BERENICE	Shut up.
BERN	He says, I can see you're not wearing any knickers. And I say, what?
BERENICE	Shut up, I can't hear.
BERN	And he says, you're not wearing knickers. I went red! How could he tell? It wasn't like I was flashing or anything.
BERENICE	Shut up!
BERN	So then I say, well, so what? And he says, I was just watching. You should be careful he says. You don't know who's looking. So I say, why should anyone be looking? And he laughed. He has a good smile. Nice strong teeth. And anyway, I say, what's it to you?
BERENICE	And what did he say?
BERN	He said maybe I'd like to find out.

BERENICE	Sounds like a creep to me.
BERN	No, he wasn't a creep. He was - different -

BERENICE kicks the television and turns it off.

BERENICE	And how old was he?
BERN	Not old. Older.
BERENICE	Personally I think there's something wrong in your head.
BERN	Jealous.
BERENICE	I don't need to walk around without knickers on to get my kicks.
BERN	You don't get any kicks at all, as far as I can see.
BERENICE	He was right. You should be careful.
BERN	It's just a bit of fun, right?
BERENICE	You might hit someone who doesn't - understand - Sometimes you worry me, Bernadette. Don't you watch the news?
BERN	You're giving me the shits now.
BERENICE	Seriously. This guy killed a woman only this week. Strangled her. It might have been that guy.
BERN	Don't be ridiculous. It's just a bit of fun.
BERENICE	Maybe that's what she thought.
	Pause.
BERN	Well, I'm seeing him tonight.
BERENICE	What?
BERN	At the movies. In public. I'm not stupid, you know.
BERENICE	Are you wearing knickers?
BERN	Who are you, my mother?
BERENICE	No, thank god.
	Pause.
	Well, are you?

BERN	Yes.
BERENICE	Do you know his name?
	Pause.
BERN	He said his name was Snoopy.
BERENICE	That's not a real name. His name. His real name.
BERN	No. What's your problem?
BERENICE	Don't go then.
BERN	What difference does it make?
BERENICE	It makes a difference.
BERN	Why?
BERENICE	You know why.
	Pause.
BERN	Fuck off. I'll see you later.

She leaves.

Scene 6

JED in the dark

JED   Assassin I acquit you in the name of rape
            Angel I acquit you in the name of atrocity
            Desire I acquit you in the name of fear
            Thief I acquit you in the name of disaster

            All is compassion
            The sun howling in his dark burrow
            The spoor of the predator
            The rose opening its petals
            To the ferocity of a single insect

            Seething multitudinous incarnadine
            Patterns of a blind order

Scene 7

The deserted fairground. Night. BERENICE

BERENICE   I have often wondered how to walk indifferently through the world. But there are issues of safety. I am a coward.

                    This fairground is beautiful. I love the huge machines standing so still and silent, the emptiness. No wilderness could be this empty. No one is laughing. No one is shooting in the gallery. No one is fighting. No one is crying. Only an evidence, a trace, in the silhouettes of the rides, the empty wrappers on the ground, the mud churned by endless feet, of something that is gone and will not be repeated.

JED becomes visible among the shadows.

JED   Everthing is repeated.

BERENICE jumps.

BERENICE   No it's not.

JED   Tomorrow the fairground will again be alive. People will tramp to the same amusements. They will repeat the same actions.

BERENICE   Different people, for different reasons.

JED   The train will go around its rails and stop, again and again. The ferris wheel will go up into the sky and down, again and again. The girls will dare each other to ride the spider and scream and be sick and drop their money. The boys will preen themselves in the shooting gallery and miss the ducks. The dodgem cars will make their endless figures of eight and parents will drive their small children, who will scream and laugh, and the teenage boy will ram the girl who makes him sweat at night and she'll think him an idiot. The tiny children will point at the train and some will be frightened and one will piss his pants.

BERENICE   It's still different.

JED   No it's not.

BERENICE   They might look the same, but they're not at all. They all come from different houses, with their own stories inside their heads.

JED   Now they're all at home.

Pause.

BERENICE   Yes.

JED   Except you. Why are you here?

BERENICE   I don't know. I wanted to see. I couldn't sleep.

JED   I live here.

BERENICE   But you couldn't sleep, either.

JED   My dreams frighten me.

BERENICE   I don't dream. Not lately.

JED   You're lucky.

BERENICE   What do you dream about?

JED   A huge horse dismembered on a beach. Its head heavy on the sand with blood streaming from its nostrils into the sea. A bird with a beak like a knife that wants to peck out my eyes. A green field and a stone church.

BERENICE   They sound beautiful.

JED   Yes.

Pause.

Have you got any plans?

BERENICE	How do you mean?
JED	What are you doing now?
BERENICE	I haven't got any plans.
JED	We could go somewhere.
BERENICE	Like where? It's late.
JED	There's places open. I know a place.
BERENICE	OK.
JED	We'll have something to drink.
BERENICE	OK.
JED	I'll tell you my dreams.
BERENICE	OK.
	Pause.
	What's your name?
	Pause.
JED	Jed.
BERENICE	That's a good name. I'm Berenice.
JED	Bringing victory.
BERENICE	What?
JED	Bringing victory. What your name means.
BERENICE	Does it? I never knew that. I don't know what Jed means.
JED	Neither do I.

They leave.

Scene 8

FLOG, drunk.

FLOG	It's always the kids. You see the kids. They're fucked before they begin. Is it their fault? It's not their fault. They're fucked already. What chance have they got?

What kind of a world is it for a kid? If I had a kid, I tell you, I'd be wondering what kind of world it is for them.

You see them on the rides. The little kids. Not a care in the world. Doughnuts and fairy floss and a ride on the kiddie train and they're laughing. But sometimes you look and you know they're fucked already. Mum and Dad wasted or strung out. A bruise on some little tacker's face. Some little girl with vomit all down her front three days old and her dress torn and her mother thin as rope and white as a sheet. But for a small while - just the smallest of whiles - those kids are somewhere else, on a train or a dragon or a horse, and they're free. Free as the air. You can see it.

There's others who don't even smile. Their faces don't change at all. All the shutters gone down inside and it's not even Monday.

I'm in the business of bringing joy into the world. Seriously. It's a serious business, see. A bit of joy. A thrill that lightens an otherwise lacklustre existence. It may be brief, but it's real.

Of course it doesn't work all the time.

I was a kid once. I was a cute little tacker. I've got photos. Of course, that was a considerable measure of time in the past.

One more the same, thanks.

Things happen to people. They do things and suddenly life isn't everything it was cracked up to be.

You get disappointed. Nothing is as real as you thought it was. Or something. You want to touch something and it wasn't really there in the first place. So it's better not to try. You give up. The world goes past you. You don't care any more because there's nothing that gives a fuck about you. That's what happens.

That's the thing about kiddies. How beautiful they are. They scramble onto the horses. Beautiful little arses and faces like angels. You could care for a kid like that, a pure thing, you could stroke his face, you could understand desire like it was before it went wrong. What it's really like. Pure. So pure you could tear it to bits just out of love. You see those kids with their mothers and your heart just swells with pity. They don't deserve that. You could care for a kid like that. You could show a kid like that what love really might be. Not a low thing, like a woman. The stink and blood and mess and tears of a female. No. Something else.

Thinking and acting. What's the difference? There's a difference? A man thinks and then he acts. A man thinks and he doesn't act. A man acts and he doesn't think. But he thought before. He thought something before, nothing comes from nothing, he thought something, even if he didn't know what it was.

He drinks in silence.

Scene 9

All night truckstop cafe. RUTH *at a table, addressing no one in particular. A* WAITER.

RUTH	Don't you fucking talk like that you arseholes. Who do you think you are? Well fuck you. Get away from me. Get away. Go away, I said. You cunts. You're cunts, I said. Fuck you.
WAITER	Hey lady.
RUTH	What?
WAITER	Keep it down.
RUTH	Fuck you too.
WAITER	Keep it down, I said. This is a public place.
RUTH	I can't see any public. Except them.
WAITER	Listen, lady. It's cool. Just keep it down.
RUTH	Do you know who I am?
WAITER	The Queen of Sheba?
RUTH	How'd you know?
WAITER	If you're the Queen of Sheba, you should mind your language.
RUTH	Mind your manners. I say what I fucking like.
WAITER	It's cool, lady, OK? I just don't want to call the cops.
RUTH	The cops? What kind of arsehole are you? Why don't you call the cops on them?
WAITER	Listen, you mad bitch -
RUTH	Don't you talk to me like that.
WAITER	All I want is for you to be quiet. I don't care what you say. Just keep it down.
RUTH	I do what I like.
WAITER	Go and do it outside then.
RUTH	It's freezing outside.
WAITER	Shut up then.

RUTH	Are you threatening me?
WAITER	Are you threatening me?
RUTH	I could wipe the floor with you, you maggot. I could - I could just - I'd -
	Pause.
	I want a doughnut.
WAITER	If you be quiet. Deal?
RUTH	OK. Be quiet, OK? OK?

JED and BERENICE enter.

JED	A coffee thanks. And?
BERENICE	One for me, too.
WAITER	On the way.

They sit down. Pause. Together:

JED	What -
BERENICE	It's very -
	Pause.
JED	I mean, it's different now.
BERENICE	What is?
JED	I know your name. You know mine. Suddenly a number of possibilities are no longer possible. Other possibilities occur.
BERENICE	Like what?
JED	I could take your hand. I could give you a new name. We could invent Arabia. We could begin a different chapter.
	Pause.
	You're shy.
BERENICE	I've always been shy. I never quite know - what to say -
JED	Shyness is charming. The reverse is - dishonest -

BERENICE	It's not dark any more.
JED	Not in here.
RUTH	Fuck off, I said. I want my doughnut.
WAITER	*(To RUTH)* What if I told them to go away?
RUTH	You could try. Arseholes!
WAITER	Piss off. Leave her alone.
BERENICE	Poor woman.
JED	I don't feel sorry for her.
RUTH	Hey, it worked! Are you a sorcerer?
WAITER	In my spare time.
RUTH	Powerful juju.
WAITER	Send your friends around. No, I didn't mean that.
JED	*(To RUTH)* Are you possessed?
RUTH	Only by the dead.

The WAITER brings the coffees and a doughnut.

WAITER	Eat your doughnut. Don't bother our clients.
JED	She's not bothering me. Which dead?
RUTH	Only the souls in the moths. I had to eat them.
JED	Right.
BERENICE	I should go home. It's getting late.
JED	Why? We only just got here.
BERENICE	I just want to go.
JED	Are you happy there? Is that why you want to go?
BERENICE	I don't know. No. It's none of your business.
JED	Do you have a boyfriend?
RUTH	You're young and pretty. You should have a boyfriend. I had a boyfriend at your age.
BERENICE	Maybe I don't want a boyfriend.
JED	Maybe you don't. Maybe you're afraid.
RUTH	I had breasts like Dolly Parton.

BERENICE	I think I'll go home.
JED	I'm not stopping you.
BERENICE	No.
JED	You could stay.
BERENICE	And then what?
JED	We could make love.
	Pause.
	I could make love to you. You could make love to me.
RUTH	Yeah, go on love.

BERENICE is mortified.

BERENICE	I think I'll go.
JED	If it makes you happy.
BERENICE	I'm not happy!
JED	Yes.
BERENICE	And neither are you.
JED	No, I'm not happy.
BERENICE	So don't talk down to me. I don't want stories. I'm tired of stories. I'm tired of making things up. I'm going home.
RUTH	You tell him, love.

She leaves.

RUTH	Pretty thing. You should be more gentle.
JED	So should you.
RUTH	You're in hell, aren't you?
JED	I guess so.
RUTH	I can tell. The voices are strong about you.
JED	Are they?
RUTH	The voices of the drowned. The girls from their

	graves. The suicides. The murdered. Those who died for love.
JED	Once you would have given me the willies.
RUTH	Not any more.
JED	No. Not any more.

Silence.

Scene 10

BERN and BERENICE.

BERN	So I waited for an hour. It was fucking freezing. But I wasn't going to go in. I didn't have enough money for a ticket. What an arsehole.
BERENICE	I warned you.
BERN	I tell you, if I see him again I'll give him a piece of my mind.
BERENICE	I'm sure it would be illuminating.
BERN	But then Ted turned up. He was just hanging out, so we went for pizza at the Frypan.
BERENICE	The world is righted once more.
BERN	I felt fucking stupid, I can tell you.
BERENICE	I did warn you.
BERN	Shut your face, Miss Smartypants. I was fucking boiling, I can tell you.
BERENICE	Maybe it was just as well.
BERN	Ted's got an old Corvette he's done up.
BERENICE	I've never really gone for motorheads.
BERN	It's really quite interesting. He had to send away for some of the parts to America. Even the doorhandles. It's taken him three years. He told me all about it.

BERENICE	Sounds fascinating.
BERN	I'm sick of this shit from you. Why don't you get a life?
BERENICE	I've been thinking about it.
BERN	You wouldn't know where to begin, would you?
BERENICE	You don't know anything.
BERN	You sit there so fucking superior and you wouldn't even dare to walk out this door.
BERENICE	Keep your pants on.
BERN	It's just jealousy.
BERENICE	Of what?
BERN	No guy would look twice at you.
BERENICE	He might.
BERN	Why would he?
BERENICE	You never know.
BERN	But you know they look at me. And you're jealous.
BERENICE	You just want me to be jealous.
BERN	I can just tell. And you put me down... because you're so shit scared...
BERENICE	Guys don't look at you, Bern. They're just looking at their own dicks.
BERN	What would you know?
BERENICE	Not as much as you, obviously.
BERN	Get fucked.
	Pause.
	You never used to be like this. You used to be nice.
BERENICE	I'm thinking of moving out.
BERN	What? Where?
BERENICE	I don't know.
BERN	You're talking crap again. You can't move out. Where would you go? What would I do?
BERENICE	What you do is your business.

Scene 11

JED and RITA

JED	Why did you come?
RITA	I came to see you.
JED	But I don't want to see you.
RITA	You were always a coward.
	Pause.
JED	Is it cold there?
RITA	Where?
JED	Where you are.
RITA	I'm here.
JED	No you're not.
RITA	I'm here, with you.
JED	But it's over.
RITA	I'll never leave you.
JED	Is that my punishment?
RITA	Yes.
JED	Then it's your punishment, as well.
RITA	Yes.
	Pause.
JED	Are you cold?
	Pause.
RITA	Strange, to see all that was me fluttering so loosely in space. And it's hard letting go of all the things I used to know myself by. To give up the meanings of a rose, the hope of a child, the continuities of time, even my own name. To know the future has no longer any human meaning. But I can't give you up. You won't let me.
JED	I got rid of you.
RITA	You bound me to you forever. I was always closer than you could admit. Now I can never grow past you. Did you hate life so much?

JED	I remember holding you in the belly of the night.
RITA	I am forgetting everything.
JED	I remember your smile in the dark. I could see the shine on your teeth. I could smell you. I was a different person then.
RITA	You are the same person. Once you could make a song to call me from the dark. But I will never return from the darkness. I can never walk into the light.
JED	Are you cold?
RITA	I am not cold. I am not warm. I am not anything.
JED	I am not anything.
RITA	That's just what you wish.
JED	What do you want?

Silence.

Scene 12

FLOG and JED.

FLOG	Almost time to go back to what's laughably called my home. A fibro shack crammed between a boot factory and a waste storage area. Very cheap and stunning industrial views.
JED	A highly desirable residence.
FLOG	I drink too much.
JED	You should get married.
FLOG	I'd only double my alcohol bill.
JED	You never know.
FLOG	She'd drink when I wasn't around. Which would be most of the time. And I'd probably drink when she was around.

JED	You'd have to change your lifestyle.
FLOG	The point is that I don't want to.
JED	I was married once.
FLOG	Yeah?
JED	It ended badly.
FLOG	Then why should I get married?
JED	Just a thought.
FLOG	I'd probably end up killing her.
JED	It's not uncommon.
FLOG	Like that arsehole who strangled his wife.
JED	A sad case.
FLOG	Neighbours said it was the last thing they expected. A lovely couple, they said. It was a shame they never had children, they said, though perhaps in the end it was all for the best.
JED	What would they know?
FLOG	He's disappeared of course. Probably drugs were involved.
JED	Probably.
FLOG	The police report they are baffled. They are entertaining a number of theories. It's always possible that he was killed as well.
JED	Highly likely, I would say.
FLOG	But it's suspicious that he disappeared. Poof! Not a trace.
JED	He probably went to Thailand. Or the Philippines. On a forged passport.
FLOG	Meeting his contacts, no doubt.
JED	Fleeing the long arm of the law. A perfidious design.
FLOG	It just goes to show you never know.
JED	Too true.
FLOG	He looked a bit like you.

JED	I've got a familiar sort of face.
FLOG	Of course, it was an old photograph.
JED	The resemblance never struck me.
FLOG	Strange you turned up the next day.
JED	You suggesting something?
FLOG	A man can put two and two together.
JED	And sometimes he comes up with five.
FLOG	Mathematics was never my strong point.
JED	Obviously.

Pause.

FLOG	You don't give a fuck about anything, do you?
JED	No.

Scene 13

Night. BERENICE at the empty fairground.

BERENICE	I came back.
	I was embarrassed.
	I'm sorry.
JED	Why? You have nothing to be sorry for.
BERENICE	Yes.
JED	What?
BERENICE	I knew something and I pretended I didn't.
JED	Everybody does that.
BERENICE	You frightened me.
JED	I frighten myself.
BERENICE	I just wanted to tell you that I knew. Something.
JED	You don't know anything.
BERENICE	There's a lot I don't know.

JED	What do you know?
BERENICE	It's hard to say.
JED	Everything is hard to say.
BERENICE	Some things are harder. You say them and the words are wrong. They nail them down and it's not nailed down at all. Words act like they know but they don't. *Pause.* You're that guy, aren't you?
JED	What guy is that?
BERENICE	The guy who killed his wife.
JED	What if I was?
BERENICE	I don't know.
JED	I could kill you.
BERENICE	I know. But you won't.
JED	How do you know?
BERENICE	I just know.
JED	You could be wrong.
BERENICE	Yes.
JED	Are you going to the police?
BERENICE	Do you think I will?
JED	No.
BERENICE	You could be wrong. *Pause.* I'm moving out of my flat. I could come with you.
JED	Where?
BERENICE	Wherever you're going.
JED	I don't need you.
BERENICE	Yes you do.
JED	You don't need me.
BERENICE	Probably.

Pause.

Why did you do it?

JED — What?

BERENICE — Why did you kill Rita?

JED — How'd you know her name?

BERENICE — I read the papers. Why?

JED — Because I'm a murderer.

BERENICE — Really why.

JED — I don't know why I did it.

BERENICE — Did you love her?

JED — Yes. No. It was - I can't say - I wasn't there - she wasn't there either - it wasn't - but we said things. Words. Photographs.

Pause.

BERENICE — What are you going to do about it?

JED — Nothing.

Kill someone else.

Nothing.

BERENICE — But you have to do something.

JED — No you don't. Somebody will do something for you. Eventually.

BERENICE — Jed.

JED — Don't call me that.

BERENICE — Jed.

JED — Don't.

BERENICE — Don't what?

JED — Don't pretend you can save me.

BERENICE — I wasn't. I was thinking something else.

JED — I'm tired of everything. Leave me alone.

BERENICE — I don't want to.

JED — I'll kill you.

BERENICE	Why?
JED	I just will. Leave me alone.
BERENICE	Half in love with easeful death.
JED	What the fuck would you know?
BERENICE	But it's not very easy.
JED	It's easier than you think.
BERENICE	How do you mean?
JED	Suddenly. Something is done. And nothing will ever make it undone. It's easier than you think.
	Pause.
BERENICE	Jed
JED	Don't call me that. Call me something else.
BERENICE	I can't think of you as anyone else.

She touches him.

	You said we could make love.
JED	So what?
	Pause.
BERENICE	I thought about you. And I understood that I knew something but it wasn't anything to do with words. And I thought that you understood that as well. But I must have been mistaken.

She begins to leave.

JED	Wait. Wait.
	Pause.
	I don't want to make anything up.

He touches her cheek. They embrace.

Scene 14

RUTH

RUTH   They went away and then they came back and then they went away again and then they came back. Policemen with wings like bats. An old man with the face of a baby. The busdriver with a hacksaw. Children with teeth like dogs. I knew what they looked like even though I never saw them. I only heard them.

They laughed at me. All of them.

They took my soul and they drew all over it with their claws. Crisscross crisscross. Teachers. Mum. The babies. The police. The judges. Crisscross crisscross. The doctors. Dad. The lawyers. The newspapers. The social workers. The nurses. The schoolkids. Crisscross crisscross. And that was my soul. This poor ragged thing where everybody walked across and tore and wrote on. They wrote everything on it. Everything. It got so I couldn't even read my own name. But then I remembered. I remembered at last.

I went down to the river to look into the water but I didn't see nothing. All the drowned girls came out and stood on the banks. They stood there shivering and they said, come in, come in. But I didn't. And they said, Ruth, come in. And I remembered my name, and I said, no. I said, no, I don't want to. I remembered my name and I said no. And that's when the trouble started.

Scene 15

BERENICE and BERN.

BERENICE   Suddenly everything makes sense. But it doesn't make any sense any more.

I wish I knew what I meant. It fits, but everything isn't what I thought. It's worse than upside down and inside out. It's stranger.

What you're told. What you believe. It's all quite different. The words don't fit. The colour's a different colour.

BERN   Have you gone crazy?
BERENICE   I don't think so.
BERN   You're talking shit.
BERENICE   No. It's just that the words don't fit.
BERN   I think you need help.
BERENICE   Help? What for?
BERN   The first sign of insanity is denial.
BERENICE   I'm trying to tell you something. I wish you'd listen.
BERN   I'm trying, I'm trying. But I think I you need to see - a counsellor, or something.
BERENICE   What could a counsellor tell me? How to go to sleep again? Here, take these pills. Here, see this doctor. What do they know about me?
BERN   They could help you.
BERENICE   I don't need help. I just - have to start again.
BERN   I don't know what you mean. Is it something I've done?
BERENICE   I'm not talking about you.
BERN   Because you should just tell me. You should just tell me to my face instead of -

BERENICE	It's not you, it's me. That's what I'm saying.
BERN	I don't know what you're talking about.
BERENICE	I know.

Scene 16

JED and RITA.

JED	It's winter. The sparrows fall frozen and starving on the ground. The sky is the colour of granite.
RITA	I know.
JED	Sometimes the sky is clear. It's a blue of immeasurable distances. I would like to go there, wherever that blue is, but I understand it is only an illusion, that it is no place, only a depth of time travelled by broken light. Light itself has no colour.
RITA	I know.
JED	Blue is the saddest colour. It symbolises how estranged one is from one's own being. If one simply was, one wouldn't have to think. One could be at home in the world. An animal can be at home in the world because it has no consciousness of its mortality. When I was a small child, I thought I would live forever. I thought the sky was a blue bowl God put over the top of the world. I don't think those things any more.
RITA	I know.
JED	Can you forgive me?
RITA	No.
JED	Will you ever forgive me?
RITA	No.

Scene 16

BERENICE and BERN. BERENICE wears a backpack. BERN has been crying.

BERN	So where are you going?
BERENICE	It doesn't have to be like this.
BERN	Why won't you give me an address?
BERENICE	I don't know what it will be.
BERN	I'll miss you. It's been years - since we were kids -
BERENICE	I'll send a postcard.
BERN	I'll miss you.
	Pause.
	Well, get out then. See if I care.
BERENICE	Goodbye.

She leaves.

Scene 17

FLOG at the fairground, packing up. BERENICE enters.

BERENICE	Excuse me.
FLOG	Yes?
BERENICE	I was wondering - I was looking for Jed.
FLOG	Jed?
BERENICE	A guy who works here. He takes tickets. On the train, I think.
FLOG	You'd be after Snoopy.
BERENICE	Snoopy?

FLOG	He had to leave.
BERENICE	Already?
FLOG	He was under some duress at the time.
BERENICE	How do you mean?
FLOG	The cops came and picked him up.
	Pause.
	They took him to the station.
	Pause.
	I don't know what it was for.
BERENICE	Oh. Did he leave anything?
FLOG	He didn't have anything.
BERENICE	Like a message or something.
FLOG	For you, you mean?
BERENICE	Maybe.
FLOG	No.
BERENICE	Oh.
FLOG	You could ask at the station.
BERENICE	I guess.
FLOG	OK then.
BERENICE	OK. Thanks.
	Pause.
	I love him
FLOG	That so?
BERENICE	But I don't know why.
FLOG	Stranger things have happened.
BERENICE	I guess I could go to the station.
FLOG	I guess that's where he is.
BERENICE	I don't think I will.
	Pause.
	Maybe later.

FLOG	Sure.
BERENICE	Maybe it would be - a tautology.
FLOG	Maybe.
BERENICE	How can you tell?
FLOG	I don't know.
BERENICE	Maybe not.
FLOG	Maybe not.
BERENICE	OK then.
FLOG	OK.

She leaves. FLOG shakes his head.

Scene 18

BERENICE on a bus. Next to her is an OLD WOMAN.

BERENICE   Assassin I acquit you in the name of death
　　　　　　Angel I acquit you in the name of rapture
　　　　　　Desire I acquit you in the name of love
　　　　　　Thief I acquit you in the name of anguish

　　　　　　All is compassion
　　　　　　The sun howling in his dark burrow
　　　　　　The spoor of the predator
　　　　　　The rose opening its petals
　　　　　　To the ferocity of a single insect

>Seething multitudinous incarnadine
>Patterns of a blind order

Silence.

WOMAN I can see you.

Blackout

Yellow

A Vampire Opera

The dead are not alive, and the living will not die. During the days when you ate what is dead, you made it come alive. When you are in the light, what will you do? On the day when you were one, you became two. But when you become two, what will you do?
                                        Gospel of Thomas, Nag Hammadi

Now women return from afar, from always: from "without", from the heath where witches are kept alive; from below, from beyond "culture"; from their childhood which men have been trying desperately to make them forget, condemning it to "eternal rest". The little girls and their "ill-mannered" bodies immured, well-preserved, intact unto themselves, in the mirror. Frigidified.
                                        The Laugh of the Medusa, Hélène Cixous

Characters: YELLOW and LAURA. They are both the same woman.

This text was written in 2017 in residence at La Chartreuse de Villeneuve lez Avignon – Centre National des Écritures du Spectacle, as part of the Odyssée-ACCR Program, with the support of the French Ministry of Culture and Communication.

First Movement

In the father's house. A ticking clock.

LAURA   It is quiet here

                Tonight the doctor and the priest came to dinner
                I listened as they talked about the world
                It is a troublesome realm

                If not for them the world would split open
                Chaos and evil would devour everything
                They sit in their black suits at the table
                And put everything in order

                I don't understand most of what they say
                There is trouble in Kyrgyzstan, Angola, Myanmar
                A murder here, a plague there, a rebellion

                They must send arms, they must attend to business
                They must bring the light of knowledge to people
                Who live in darkness and sorrow

                They are great men and they are kind to me
                They bring me flowers and books and toys
                The priest and the doctor flirt with me
                As if I were their own daughter

                My father smiles gravely and sends me to bed
                Laura, he says, you wouldn't understand
                Laura, he says, we must put things in order
                You mustn't worry your pretty head

> If not for them the world would split open
> Chaos and evil would devour everything
> They sit in their black suits at the table
> And put everything in order

Moonlit curtains.

> It is quiet here
> I am utterly alone
> In my white room
>
> The house breathes beneath me like a great beast
> Guarding me from sorrow and chaos
>
> The moon shines through the windows
> Like a woman in a shroud
>
> I'm alone but I'm not lonely
> Because I am perfectly happy
> In my father's house

A dog howls. LAURA starts up in her bed. YELLOW appears outside the window behind her.

YELLOW   I am desire returned from death

> No walls can contain me
> No door can shut me out
>
> Your fathers murdered me
> One after the other

>   Mutilating my beauty
>   Into the shapes of their own fear
>
>   They hold up my bleeding head
>   And claim that I am the monster
>
>   But look, for you my hands are gentle
>   For you my voice is low

LAURA   Mama? Mama!

YELLOW stares at her, hungry.

YELLOW   They have told my story
                Again and again
                They hold the mirror to my absent face
                They draw me in blood
                They name me death
                They fear the darkness
                Because I walk inside it
                They say I must be punished

                I am not their monster

LAURA turns and sees YELLOW.

Second Movement

LAURA rises from her bed.

LAURA   Oh mother protect me
                I don't remember my mother's face she dissolved
                Silently into the vapours of my childhood
                I don't remember her voice

YELLOW   I can see her footprint, a faint mark on stone
                Painstakingly erased

LAURA   There is no image of my mother in this house
                Sometimes my father speaks of her
                His face heavy with sorrow

YELLOW   She suckled me on her blood
                She laboured in anguish
                To bring me into the world

LAURA   I will never match her goodness
                She was patient and endlessly loving
                Her hands folded in submission
                Like an angel

YELLOW   Her blood is wiped clean now
                Her madness is forgotten

LAURA   She blooms forever young
                In the crypt of his memory

YELLOW   Her scream in the night
                    Was a red flag of pain

LAURA   Through tangled fingers I see the edge
                    Of things, perilous and strange.

                    Outside these walls are monsters.
                    My father tells me to be wary.

                    Be careful, Laura. Don't go there. Don't.
                    I don't go there.

                    Stay here where my shadow
                    Divides your face.

                    It's safe here, clean as your girlhood.
                    Pure. White. Pure.

YELLOW   You are not pure
                    You were never pure
                    Nothing can live in purity

LAURA   In this light my skin might be as smooth as plastic
                    That lets nothing through, not one molecule
                    Of taint

                    Odourless and without texture
                    Such perfection, admire me

YELLOW   You are the mannequin of their dreams, they move
                    Each limb into the shape of their lust

You demand nothing, the slave of their pleasure
They watch your eyes observing them watching you

Die in their gaze, to be reborn again and again
Beautiful, obedient, undead

They see only your skin
The reflection in your eyes
That reflects only them

LAURA   They see only my skin
But inside and outside is a storm
Vortices of pleasure
That I dare not name

YELLOW   They see only their reflection
And then it is too late
I smash the mirror and step through
A monster

YELLOW vanishes. LAURA runs to the window.

Third Movement

A doorway. YELLOW and LAURA on either side. A storm rising.

YELLOW   There is always a storm
                  Leaves flying through the yellow air
                  Black branches thrashing

                  The street is empty
                  I walk alone through the singing dark
                  I knock on the door

                  You invite me in

TOGETHER   When I saw you in the doorway
                  Worlds shuddered to a halt

                  Yellow and Laura, Laura and Yellow
                  Two mirrors doubled to infinity

YELLOW   Your skin is a threshold

LAURA   Close the door I am frightened

YELLOW   Your eyes are a window

LAURA   I am blind I am frightened

YELLOW   Your mouth is an abyss

LAURA   An abyss of tears an abyss of blood

YELLOW   See how I shiver with love for you
            See how I swoon for your beauty

LAURA   I am drowning I am dying

            I see the blood crowd in your lips
            I see the flame in your pupil
            My body trembles

            Stay hidden, tiny flame
            stay out of the light

            If you are seen
            I will collapse to ash
            in the white glare of my father

YELLOW   I will eat you whole
            Unlatch your tongue and lift out your eyes from your
                skull
            Untie your lips from your face

            I'll tenderly loose your limbs one joint from the other
            Unwrap the shimmering treasures of your belly
            Suck each finger to the bone

            I'll gorge myself on your gelatinous flesh
            Each fragrant drop of your juices

            Your body is a feast
            Nothing disgusts me

LAURA   Eat me Yellow eat me

Fourth Movement

The father's house. YELLOW and LAURA.

YELLOW   He says child, what is this languor?
                 She says father I am bleeding

LAURA   He says, why are your lips so red?
                 I say, father I am bleeding

YELLOW   He says, why is your glance so wild?
                 What is this pallor in your cheek?
                 Your pulse, it is so fast

LAURA   Father, I am bleeding

YELLOW   He frowns he can't quite hear her
                 He takes her temperature
                 He checks her pulse

LAURA   He is frowning he is worried
                 I laugh and bite my lips
                 He cannot see inside me

YELLOW   He calls the doctor to his house
                 They whisper in the corner
                 They are frowning they are worried

LAURA   They speak in gentle voices
                 They say, Laura, can you hear me?
                 They say, Laura, take this pill
                 I know they love me they'll not harm me

YELLOW   They shake their heads they say
         There must be some contamination
         A bad air a malignity
         A black madness in the blood

LAURA   I know he loves me he'll not harm me

YELLOW   When she gags they ram the pill down
         When she struggles they bind her
         When she tries to run they lock her up
         When she weeps they call the priest
         To pray for her

LAURA   I am a sick animal
         I see the shame in their eyes
         I have dishonoured them

         They speak in gentle voices
         They say, Laura, can you hear me?
         They say, Laura, take this pill
         Or worse will follow
         Oh yes much worse will follow

LAURA faints.

YELLOW   They will make you forget me
         All the pollen of my touch
         Will fall to acid earth

         I will walk in the night
         In a hood of blood
         I will sharpen my teeth
         On my bitterness

I will tear that white shroud
Until you remember your mongrel colours
Your dappled beauty your dark sex
Your own complex voice

Fifth Movement

A cemetery. LAURA lies in a coffin. YELLOW amid the gravestones.

YELLOW   The moon is shrouded like a dead woman
Who walks alone in the bruised shadows
Blood clotting in her veins

The doctor the priest and the father say
They must put things in order

The night embraces them with rotting limbs
They shudder as their flesh melts in answer
The darkness sings and they pray in terror

The doctor the priest and the father say
Righteousness will protect them
Nothing will escape their revenge

They bury their nightmares deep
In the grave of their crippled lust
Where rotting lilies exhale
Their corrupt sensual perfumes

They are saving Laura from herself
Here is the stake to pierce her heart
Here is the axe

LAURA screams and rises up in terror.

LAURA   They stand above me in their black suits
         To put everything in order

         Their faces are neither dead nor living
         I see the lust in their eyes

         They'll stake me to the sterile ground
         They'll hack off my head
         And I will forget everything

Blinding light. The shadows are banished.

YELLOW   The moon is a woman in a silver dress
         Her face is as black as your own heart

         Look how she stoops and blinds them
         Look how their laws collapse before her
         Look how she steps out of the sky
         And lifts you into her arms

Yellow takes Laura's hand and leads her out of the coffin.

LAURA   Yellow I've been so lonely
         In the silent rooms
         Of my father's house

YELLOW   The moon wants you to sing

They sing together.

Epilogue

LAURA and YELLOW. They are in another place.

LAURA   My father's house is scrubbed clean
Not one drop of blood
Not one smear no stain no smell
I am no longer there

YELLOW   You are no longer there
We stand outside the walls
Waiting for the dawn

LAURA   All those years ago they saved my mother

YELLOW   All those years ago they murdered her

BOTH (as desired – may be chanted or spoken)

LAURA   My mother
Who stumbled the hallway her brain on fire drugged hysterical weeping
Clutching the scars where they ripped her womb where her sex was burned with righteousness
Who counted the wounds her mouth her breasts her bones her fingers all the luminous damage
Who trembled in the electric wires who spat when they called it sanity
Who bled on the walls as they pounded glorious reason into her body

                Who vomited on the spotless sheets who tore her face and slashed the stitches open who bit her hands and screamed
                Through the long intolerable loathsome crucifixions of shame

YELLOW   Our mothers
               Who crippled their hands with invisible labour and rose each morning to do it again
                Who wrote their bitter secrets over and over in the book of erasures
                Who broke the windows who smashed the locks who screamed their madness into the pitiless night
                Raped in alleys and marital bedrooms in ditches and universities in slums and offices and churches silenced under the law
                Falling nameless and unforgiven in crowded streets and empty hostels in cities and dumps and forgotten precincts in all the meadows of killing

BOTH   Our mother
                Whose tongue was bees whose limbs were forbidden honey
                Whose eyes snapped open like the lid of the sun who said become and become
                From all the pores of her blossoming skin from all her colours from all her hidden shapes and languages
                Who raised her criminal fist to the sterile sky who sobbed her criminal tears who opened her criminal mouth and screamed no more
                Who burst out of the coffin where they hammered her in and said I am no monster

>   Who said I am no part of your monstrous house
>   Who stepped out of the laws of death and said you
>   cannot kill me

The sun begins to rise.

YELLOW   They cannot bury us deep enough
            We will always return

LAURA   My father's house is clean and empty
            All day long he stares with his hollow eyes
            Trembling in the dark

BOTH   And we stand in the sun

They embrace.

www.ingramcontent.com/pod-product-compliance
Lightning Source LLC
Chambersburg PA
CBHW031424290426
44110CB00011B/518